Contents

Land of riches

The country of Mexico is on the continent of North America. It shares its northern border with the United States and its southern border with Guatemala and Belize. Mexico's west coast lies on the Pacific Ocean, and its east coast on the Gulf of Mexico. The tropical sun warms southern Mexico, bringing hot, humid weather. The drier north is covered by deserts. High snowy mountains slope down to low sandy coasts. Rich farmland bursts with crops.

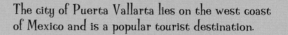

The city of Puerta Vallarta lies on the west coast of Mexico and is a popular tourist destination.

Global Cookery

en Rau

Raintree is an imprint of Capstone Global Library Limited, a company incorporated in England and Wales having its registered office at 7 Pilgrim Street, London, EC4V 6LB – Registered company number: 6695582

www.raintreepublishers.co.uk
myorders@raintreepublishers.co.uk

Text © Capstone Global Library Limited 2014
First published in hardback in 2014
Paperback edition first published in 2015
The moral rights of the proprietor have been asserted.

Edited by Abby Colich, Laura Knowles, and John-Paul Wilkins
Designed by Cynthia Akiyoshi
Picture research by Tracy Cummins
Production by Vicki Fitzgerald
Originated by Capstone Global Library
Printed and bound in China

ISBN 978 1 406 27382 3 (hardback)
17 16 15 14 13
10 9 8 7 6 5 4 3 2 1

ISBN 978 1 406 27387 8 (paperback)
18 17 16 15 14
10 9 8 7 6 5 4 3 2 1

A full catalogue record for this book is available from the British Library.

Acknowledgments
The author and publisher are grateful to the following for permission to reproduce copyright material: Capstone Publishers pp. 1, 9–11, 16–43 (Karon Dubke); © Crown p.12 (copyright material is reproduced with the permission of HMSO and Queen's Printer for Scotland, food.gov.uk); Getty Images pp. 6 (Stuart Antrobus), 7 (Fuse), 13 (Juanmonino), 15 (Barry Austin Photography); Shutterstock pp. 4 (Anton_Ivanov), 5 (ChameleonsEye), 14 (Gayvoronskaya_Yana).

Design elements reproduced with permission of Shutterstock (Fedorov Oleksiy, Luis Santos, Mazzzur, Nattika, Richard Peterson, Stephen B. Goodwin, Boris15, Brooke Becker, Manuel Fernandes, marchello74, photastic, photomatz, Picsfive, Reinhold Leitner, Sandra Cunningham, yeray lapuente chico).

Cover photograph of steak tacos reproduced with permission of Capstone Publishers (Karon Dubke).

We would like to thank Dr. Monica A. Rankin, Sarah Schenker, and Marla Conn for their invaluable help in the preparation of this book.

Every effort has been made to contact copyright holders of material reproduced in this book. Any omissions will be rectified in subsequent printings if notice is given to the publishers.

Over thousands of years, small farming villages of the region developed into great civilizations, such as the Olmec, Maya, and Aztec. Spanish explorers in the Caribbean area set out for Mexico and arrived in 1519 looking for gold and treasure. They came in contact with the Aztecs, a powerful and rich empire. After violent battles, the Spanish took over. After three centuries under colonial rule, Mexicans fought for independence. This was finally achieved in 1821.

Traditional music is part of Mexico's rich culture.

Today, most Mexicans are related to both the Spanish and the native peoples of the past. Most Mexicans speak Spanish. But some hold on to the original traditions and languages of their ancestors. In big cities, people might live in high-rise buildings. In the country, homes of sun-baked adobe bricks blend in with the land. All over the country, people gather in the marketplace (*mercado*) to enjoy the riches of Mexico's land.

5

Combining two cultures

What does Mexican food make you think of? Tacos, crunchy tortilla chips, and spicy salsa? These are classic Mexican foods. But in Mexico, there is a much greater variety of ingredients and flavours.

Street vendors sell refreshing snacks of sweet fruit to help customers cool off on a hot day.

Two traditions combined into the dishes we now call Mexican food – one was from the ancient peoples who lived in the area long ago, and the other was from Spanish settlers. As early as 7,000 BC, the people of the region grew tomatoes, peppers (*chillies*), beans, avocados, squash, and most importantly, corn. Corn was, and still is, the basis of the Mexican diet. Chocolate and vanilla are also native to the area. The Spaniards brought new foods, such as meat (from livestock), cheese, rice, and wheat.

Within Mexico, however, not all food is the same. In the north, where ranchers raise cattle, lots of dishes include beef and cheese. In central Mexico, nuts, spices, and chocolate make their way into many meals. On the southern coasts, fish and shellfish are common.

A typical day for most Mexicans starts with a small breakfast, called *desayuno*. Then they might eat a heartier meal, *almuerzo*, in the late morning. The biggest meal of the day, *comida*, is traditionally served in the afternoon. Later at night, Mexicans might eat a light supper called *cena*.

Food and family are deeply rooted in Mexican culture.

If you are hungry for a snack in Mexico, you might stop at a *taqueria*. At these shops, you can pick up portable treats, such as tamales (cornmeal steamed inside corn husks), quesadillas (tortillas folded around fillings), or tacos – for which Mexico is so well known.

7

Mexican ingredients

Here are some ingredients found in Mexican households and in the recipes in this book. If you can't find a certain ingredient, look for similar replacements.

Corn is the basis for many meals. Mexicans grind up dried corn to make dough for tortillas. The husks are used as a wrapping for tamales. The kernels are dried to make hominy, an ingredient added to stews.

Tortillas are flat breads that accompany most meals in Mexico. They are made fresh daily. Most Mexicans eat corn tortillas, but in the north, where farms grow wheat, you will find flour tortillas as well.

Tomatoes and avocados are often used in the condiments salsa and guacamole.

Chilli peppers come fresh or dried and in many sizes, colours, and levels of heat. Fresh chilli peppers include bell peppers, poblano, jalapeño, serrano, and habanero. Dried poblano peppers are called ancho or pasilla. Dried jalapeños become chipotles. Dried peppers can be ground into powders or soaked until soft before being added to a dish.

Beans come with many Mexican meals. Pinto, red kidney, and black beans are just a few types.

Rice is served along with many meals as well. The most common type in Mexico is medium-grain rice.

Herbs and spices include coriander, epazote, oregano, and cinnamon. Vanilla flavour comes from the tiny seeds of an orchid plant.

Cheeses are often used as a condiment on street foods. Crumbly queso fresco is one of the most popular. Stringy asadero is good for melting. Mild feta can be used in place of queso fresco and Monterey Jack in place of asadero.

Chocolate is native to Mexico. It comes from the seeds of the cacao pod and is traditionally used for drinking.

Fruit grows well in Mexico's tropical climate. Some of the most popular Mexican fruits are bananas, pineapples, mangoes, papayas, and guavas. Citrus fruits also add flavour to dishes. Prickly pear fruit grows on the prickly pear cactus. Cherimoya is a unique fruit that tastes like a combination of banana, papaya, and pineapple.

Other fruits and vegetables include jicama (a beetroot-shaped root vegetable), chayote squash, squash blossoms, cactus paddles (*nopales*), and radishes. Many dishes are flavoured with onions and garlic. Tomatillos look like small, unripe tomatoes, but they are actually relatives of the gooseberry.

Seeds and nuts, such as pumpkin seeds (*pepitas*), pecans, walnuts, peanuts, and coconuts, add flavour to Mexican dishes.

Meat, poultry, and seafood include beef and pork, chicken and turkey, red snapper, crabs, and prawns. Chorizo is a famous Mexican sausage seasoned with chillies.

The Mexican diet contains lots of delicious, fresh ingredients.

How to use this book

Each chapter of this book will introduce you to aspects of Mexican cooking. But you don't have to read the book from beginning to end. Flip through, find what interests you, and give it a try. You may discover a recipe that becomes your new favourite meal!

Steak tacos

Tacos are perfectly designed as street food. These soft corn tortillas, packed with many varieties of beef, pork, chicken, eggs, beans, potatoes, prawns, or chorizo, are easy to eat from your hand. *Carne asada*, or grilled meat, is a popular taco filling.

Ingredients

450 g flank steak (or any boneless steak)
2 cloves garlic, minced
Juice of 2 limes
Salt and pepper to taste
1 tablespoon vegetable oil
Corn tortillas

Garnishes, including salsa, guacamole, sliced radishes, and grated cheese

Tools

Kitchen scales
Measuring spoons
Knife
Chopping board
Cling film
Bowl
Frying pan
Spatula
Microwave (optional)

If you already do a lot of cooking, you may know your way around the kitchen. But if you've never roasted a pepper, sautéed chorizo, or pureed tomatoes, don't worry. Have a look at the glossary on page 44.

24

Each recipe is set up the same way: Ingredients lists all the ingredients you'll be adding. Tools tells you the various kitchen utensils you will need. Collect the ingredients and tools before you start working so that you have everything nearby when you need it.

Then just follow the Steps. Make sure you read them carefully. Numbers on the photos indicate which step they refer to. Don't worry if your creation isn't perfect when you reach the end. Cooking takes practice and experimentation. Be patient and enjoy the process.

If you have to follow a specific diet, or have food allergies, look for the labels on each recipe. These will tell you if a dish is vegan, vegetarian, dairy-free, gluten-free, or if it contains nuts. However, you should always check food packaging before use to be sure.

Steps

1. Cut the steak into 4 to 6 pieces. Place in a bowl. Add the garlic, lime juice, salt, and pepper. Mix together, cover with cling film, and then marinate in the refrigerator for about 30 minutes.

2. Heat the oil in a frying pan over medium-high heat. Place the steak in the pan. Cook for about 5 to 7 minutes on one side. Flip over and cook for about 5 minutes more (cooking time will depend on the thickness of the meat). Set aside.

3. Prepare your garnishes (see page 34 for salsa and page 36 for guacamole). Heat the tortillas in a pan or in the microwave (see Quick tip on page 19).

4. Cut the meat into strips. Place a few strips inside each tortilla and add the toppings of your choice.

Quick tips

Mincing means to cut an ingredient into tiny pieces. To make mincing garlic easier, you can use a garlic press. The press will mince the garlic for you.

Making tacos can be as much fun as eating them. Serve the meal as a taco buffet – set out a stack of tortillas, bowls of the meat, and bowls of each topping. Let your guests make their own tacos with their favourite garnishes.

VARIATION

Tacos are a good way to use up leftover meat. Shred up cooked chicken or chop up leftover pork or steak. Warm it in a frying pan with some onions and chilli peppers for a tasty taco filling.

Makes 4 servings
Time: About 1 hour

25

N uts contains

D airy free

G luten free

V egetarian

V egan

Look at Quick tips for cooking and kitchen advice, and Variations for swapping out ingredients for others if you would like.

Whenever you are in the kitchen, ask an adult to help or be nearby. You shouldn't use any knife or appliance without an adult's permission and assistance. You can find more ways to be safe while you cook on page 14.

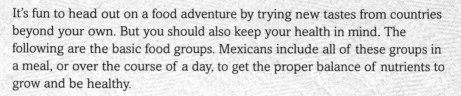

A healthy kitchen

It's fun to head out on a food adventure by trying new tastes from countries beyond your own. But you should also keep your health in mind. The following are the basic food groups. Mexicans include all of these groups in a meal, or over the course of a day, to get the proper balance of nutrients to grow and be healthy.

Fruits and vegetables

Tropical bananas, pineapples, and mangoes are sweet. Squirts of lime in salsa and guacamole add zing. Chillies, tomatoes, and tomatillos top the list of popular vegetables in Mexico. Squash and cactus paddles are common, too. Both fruits and vegetables can help reduce the risk of getting certain diseases. They contain nutrients your body needs and fibre to keep your digestive system running smoothly.

Grains

These are foods made from wheat, rice, corn, or other grains. Whole grains that use the entire grain kernel are the healthiest. Refined grains, such as white flour and white rice, do not have as many vitamins and minerals. Rice is a common Mexican grain, but corn has always been the main grain of Mexico.

The eatwell plate shows us the importance of eating a combination of all the food groups in our diets.

Guacamole is a delicious dish filled with healthy vegetables. You can find a recipe for guacamole on page 36.

Protein

Protein foods include meat, poultry, seafood, and eggs. Steak tacos, mole with chicken, and ranchers' eggs all contain protein. A popular source of protein for Mexicans is beans.

Dairy

Milk and any products made from milk fall into this category. Dairy foods contain a lot of bone-building calcium. But cheeses also contain a lot of fat. So try not to overload your taco. Choose low-fat options when you can – Mexican hot chocolate is just as tasty with skimmed milk as with semi-skimmed or whole milk.

Fats and sugar

Some oils, especially the ones from plants, like vegetable oil, do provide some important nutrients. Nuts are high in oils, too. Avocados contain healthy fats. But solid fats, such as butter and meat fat, are not as good for you. So use them sparingly. Your body needs sugar, but not too much. Try not to fill up on too many Mexican sweets!

A safe kitchen

It's fun to whip up a tasty new creation in the kitchen, but safety should be your number one concern. Here are some tips to keep in mind:

- Make sure an adult is nearby for permission, help, advice, and assistance.
- Wash your hands before you work.
- Wear the right clothing, including sturdy shoes and an apron.
- Foods can grow harmful bacteria. Make sure you keep foods in the refrigerator or freezer until they are ready to use. Check expiration dates. If something smells or looks funny, it may be spoiled.

Always wash your hands and chopping boards after handling raw meat.

Be careful when using the oven. Wear oven gloves to protect your hands from burns.

- Raw meat, poultry, seafood, and eggs can carry germs. Always wash your hands immediately after touching them. Wash any knife or chopping board after you use them with these foods. Make sure these foods are cooked all the way through before you eat them. Clean countertops and kitchen tools with warm, soapy water when you have finished working.

- On the hob, make sure pan handles point in, so the pans don't get knocked over. Never leave pans unattended. Do not let anything flammable, such as loose sleeves or tea towels, near burners on the hob.

- Always use oven gloves when removing something from the oven or microwave. Avoid steam when you lift a top off a pan on the hob or in the oven.

- Knives are sharp. Always point the blade away from you. Take your time and pay attention to what you are cutting. Don't use a knife without the help of an adult.

Por la mañana (In the morning)

The first meal of the day is *desayuno* – a light breakfast of fruit, rolls, and a warm drink or juice. But after working up an appetite later in the morning, some Mexicans might have a second, more substantial breakfast. This meal might include an egg dish, beans, and of course, tortillas.

Atole

Atole is made from a very finely ground cornflour, called masa harina, that is cooked until smooth and sweetened with sugar and spices. Mexicans sometimes save atole for special occasions, such as the Day of the Dead or Christmas. You can drink this thick drink hot, or cool it to room temperature.

Ingredients

240 ml water
240 ml milk
3 tablespoons masa harina
¼ teaspoon ground cinnamon
2 tablespoons brown sugar
½ teaspoon vanilla extract

Tools

Measuring jug and spoons
Stockpot or saucepan
Whisk
Mugs

Steps

1. Heat the water and milk in a stockpot on medium-high. While it's heating, whisk in the masa harina, cinnamon, brown sugar, and vanilla.

2. When it starts to bubble, turn the heat down. Cook for about 5 minutes, stirring frequently, to make sure the masa harina does not stick to the bottom.

3. Remove from heat and pour into mugs to serve.

Makes 2 servings
Time: About 10 minutes

luten free egetarian

VARIATION

Champurrado is chocolate atole. When the atole is warmed through, take it off the heat, and add about 50 g of dark chocolate chips. Whisk together until the chocolate is melted.

Ranchers' eggs

Mexican cowboys have a long tradition of working hard on ranches. They protect and care for the cattle. This hearty dish, *huevos rancheros*, gave them the energy to work from morning to night. Try this dish when you have to get ready for an especially busy day!

Ingredients

100 g red salsa (see recipe on page 34)
2 corn tortillas
4 large eggs

Tools

Kitchen scales
Blender
Saucepan
Frying pan
Spatula
Plates

Steps

1. In a blender, puree the salsa into a smooth sauce. Heat the sauce in a small saucepan over medium heat for about 5 minutes to warm it through.

2. Heat the frying pan on medium-high. Warm the tortillas in the pan, about 15 seconds for each side. Set aside.

3. Crack the eggs into the pan. Cook for about 3 minutes on one side. Flip and cook for about 2 minutes more.

4. On each plate, stack one tortilla, two eggs, and top with the warm salsa.

Quick tip

There are a few ways to warm tortillas:

- Warm them for 15 seconds each side in a hot pan.

- Wrap them in a moist kitchen roll, and heat for 45 seconds in the microwave.

- Wrap them in foil and heat for 3 minutes in a 120°C oven.

Makes 2 servings
Time: 10 minutes

Vegetarian

19

Hot chocolate

The Olmec, Maya, and Aztec cultures of Mexico's history valued the cacao plant. Cacao beans were ground to make a warm chocolate drink. Beans were so valuable that the Aztecs used them as money.

Chocolate is not naturally sweet. The chips used in this recipe have sugar added to them. Mexicans use a traditional tool, called a *molinillo*, to whip the hot chocolate. You can use a blender to make it frothy.

Ingredients	Tools
500 ml milk	Kitchen scales
½ teaspoon ground cinnamon (or 1 cinnamon stick)	Measuring jug and spoons
	Stockpot or saucepan
⅛ teaspoon almond extract	Mixing spoon
75 g dark chocolate chips	Handheld blender
	Towel
	Mugs

Steps

1. Heat the milk, cinnamon, and almond extract in a stockpot on medium for about 3 to 5 minutes until hot (not boiling).

2. Add the chocolate and stir for about 2 to 3 minutes more until it dissolves.

3. Remove the stockpot from the heat. Blend until frothy with a handheld blender.

4. Pour into mugs to serve.

Quick tip

If you don't have a handheld blender, you can use a normal blender. Keep the lid off to let steam escape, but cover it with a towel in case it splashes.

 Ncontains uts

 Gluten free (with gluten-free chocolate)

Vegetarian

Makes 2 servings
Time: About 10 minutes

Cocinar con carne (Cooking with meat)

Before the Spaniards arrived, the Mexican diet included tomatoes, corn, chillies, and beans. They kept turkeys and ducks for food. But the Spanish explorers introduced beef, chicken, and pork. These dishes represent some of Mexico's popular meat meals.

Molten cheese casserole

This bubbling cheesy northern dish, called *queso fundido*, is tastiest straight from the oven. It can be used as a filling for tortillas. You can also enjoy it as a dip for crunchy tortilla chips. Jalapeños or bell peppers can be used if poblanos are hard to find.

Ingredients

1 poblano pepper
 (or 1 bell pepper, or
 2 jalapeños)
225 g Monterey Jack
 cheese (or mild
 cheddar), grated
225 g chorizo

Tools

Grill pan
Paper bag and clip
Knife
Chopping board
Frying pan
Mixing spoon

Kitchen roll
Plate
Grater
Baking dish

Steps

1. To roast the pepper, place it on a grill pan. Grill the pepper on high for about 15 to 20 minutes. Turn it frequently during cooking so that the skin is completely charred on all sides.

2. Place the pepper in a paper bag and clip the top closed. Let it sit for 15 minutes.

3. Run the pepper under cold water while you peel off the skin and remove the stem, seeds, and inner veins. Drain it on some kitchen roll. Then slice it into strips and set aside.

4. Preheat oven to 180°C.

5. Squeeze the chorizo out of its casing into a frying pan and break it up with a spoon into small pieces. Cook the chorizo on a medium-high heat for about 10 to 15 minutes until it is browned and cooked through. Drain on a plate lined with some kitchen roll.

6. In a baking dish, combine the chorizo, peppers, and cheese.

7. Bake for 10 to 15 minutes until the cheese is melted and bubbly.

Quick tip

Hot chilli peppers add spiciness to your dishes. But you have to be safe when you handle them. Rubber gloves are good protection against the peppers' oils. These oils can get on your skin. If you should touch your face after working with chillies, you might burn your eyes. When you have finished seeding and slicing up peppers, wash your hands well with warm soapy water.

Gluten free
(with gluten-free chorizo)

Makes 4 to 6 servings
Time: About 1 hour

Steak tacos

Tacos are perfectly designed as street food. These soft corn tortillas, packed with many varieties of beef, pork, chicken, eggs, beans, potatoes, prawns, or chorizo, are easy to eat from your hand. *Carne asada*, or grilled meat, is a popular taco filling.

Ingredients

450 g flank steak (or any boneless steak)

2 cloves garlic, minced

Juice of 2 limes

Salt and pepper to taste

1 tablespoon vegetable oil

Corn tortillas

Garnishes, including salsa, guacamole, sliced radishes, and grated cheese

Tools

Kitchen scales

Measuring spoons

Knife

Chopping board

Cling film

Bowl

Frying pan

Spatula

Microwave (optional)

Steps

1. Cut the steak into 4 to 6 pieces. Place in a bowl. Add the garlic, lime juice, salt, and pepper. Mix together, cover with cling film, and then marinate in the refrigerator for about 30 minutes.

2. Heat the oil in a frying pan over medium-high heat. Place the steak in the pan. Cook for about 5 to 7 minutes on one side. Flip over and cook for about 5 minutes more (cooking time will depend on the thickness of the meat). Set aside.

3. Prepare your garnishes (see page 34 for salsa and page 36 for guacamole). Heat the tortillas in a pan or in the microwave (see Quick tip on page 19).

4. Cut the meat into strips. Place a few strips inside each tortilla and add the toppings of your choice.

Quick tips

Mincing means to cut an ingredient into tiny pieces. To make mincing garlic easier, you can use a garlic press. The press will mince the garlic for you.

Making tacos can be as much fun as eating them. Serve the meal as a taco buffet – set out a stack of tortillas, bowls of the meat, and bowls of each topping. Let your guests make their own tacos with their favourite garnishes.

VARIATION

Tacos are a good way to use up leftover meat. Shred up cooked chicken or chop up leftover pork or steak. Warm it in a frying pan with some onions and chilli peppers for a tasty taco filling.

Makes 4 servings
Time: About 1 hour

Tortilla soup

This classic Mexican soup is a good way to bring stale tortillas back to life. A warm chicken stock makes this a cozy, comforting meal. In Mexico, round corn tortillas would be deep-fried to make them crunchy. Here we use dry tortilla chips instead.

Ingredients

1 tablespoon vegetable oil

3 large tomatoes cut into chunks

1 medium onion, cut into chunks

2 cloves garlic, peeled

2 tablespoons chopped green chillies (or to taste)

Salt and pepper, to taste

1.3 litres chicken stock

Tortilla chips

Queso fresco, mild feta, or mild cheddar cheese

Lime wedges

1 avocado, cubed

Tools

Measuring jug and spoons

Stockpot

Mixing spoon

Handheld blender

Knife

Chopping board

Bowls

Ladle

Steps

1. In a stockpot, heat oil over medium-high heat. Cook the tomato, onion, garlic, and chilli for about 15 minutes until softened.

2. Remove mixture from the heat and puree until smooth with a handheld blender. Alternatively, you can use a normal blender (see Quick tip on page 21). Return the puree to the heat and cook for about 5 minutes. Add salt and pepper to taste.

3. Add the chicken stock and bring to the boil. Turn the heat down, and then simmer for about 20 to 30 minutes.

4. Crush the tortillas into small pieces. Place the tortillas and a sprinkle of cheese in the bottom of each bowl. Ladle the soup over the tortillas and cheese.

5. Garnish with cubes of avocado and lime wedges.

VARIATION

When you add the chicken stock, you can also add about a cup of cooked, shredded chicken to make the soup a little heartier.

Makes 4 servings
Time: About 1 hour

27

Mole with chicken

Mole sauce has a long history in Mexico. Moles are known for their long list of ingredients, including fruits, nuts, chillies, and chocolate. These are combined into a smooth sauce that is served with chicken, or more traditionally, turkey. Mole is made with dried chillies, but you can use chilli powder instead. Serve it with Mexican rice (see recipe on page 30).

Ingredients

700 g boneless, skinless chicken thighs

30 g almonds

50 g raisins

1 tablespoon sesame seeds

3 tablespoons chilli powder

3 tablespoons unsweetened cocoa powder

½ teaspoon ground cinnamon

⅛ teaspoon ground cloves

2 tablespoons sugar

1 teaspoon salt

¼ teaspoon pepper

1 tortilla, shredded

1 tablespoon vegetable oil

½ medium onion

2 cloves garlic, minced

1 (400-g) tin chopped tomatoes

Tools

Kitchen scales

Measuring spoons

Blender

Frying pan

Mixing spoon

Baking dish

Steps

1. Preheat oven to 190°C.

2. In a blender, combine the almonds, raisins, sesame seeds, chilli powder, cocoa powder, cinnamon, cloves, sugar, salt and pepper, and the shredded tortilla.

3. Heat the oil in a frying pan on medium-high. Sauté the onion for about 6 to 8 minutes. Add the garlic and sauté for 1 to 2 minutes more.

4. Add the onion, garlic, and the chopped tomatoes to the blender with the other ground ingredients. Blend until the sauce is smooth.

5. Put the chicken into a baking dish. Pour the sauce over the chicken and mix together. Bake uncovered for about 30 minutes until the chicken is cooked through and the sauce is hot and bubbly.

Makes 4 servings
Time: About 1 hour

Nuts contains

Con la comida (With the meal)

Mexican meals are tasty. But side dishes and accompaniments also add lots of flavour. Many dishes would feel incomplete without rice, beans, salsa, and guacamole.

Mexican rice

Rice is not native to Mexico. It was brought over by the Spaniards. But it has been made uniquely Mexican by the addition of chillies and tomatoes. Instead of steaming the rice, Mexicans fry it in oil first. Mexican rice is sometimes called "red rice".

Ingredients

2 large tomatoes, seeded and diced (about 400 g)
1 tablespoon vegetable oil
½ medium onion, diced
2 cloves garlic, minced
450 ml chicken stock
Salt, to taste
200 g medium-grain white rice
2 tablespoons chopped green chillies (or to taste)
50 g frozen peas, thawed

Tools

Kitchen scales
Chopping board
Knife
Measuring jug and spoons
Stockpot
Mixing spoon

Steps

1. Heat the oil in the stockpot over medium-high heat. Add the rice and cook for about 3 minutes until it begins to brown. Add the onion and garlic, and cook for about 5 minutes more.

2. Add the chillies, stock, tomatoes, and salt. Bring to the boil, reduce the heat, and simmer covered for 15 minutes.

3. Stir the peas into the rice, cover, and cook for about 5 minutes more until the peas are cooked through. Serve warm as part of a main meal.

Gluten free
(with gluten-free stock cubes)

Dairy free

Makes 4 to 6 servings
Time: About 40 minutes

Refried beans

Beans are served with most meals in Mexico. Pinto beans are more common in the north, and black beans are more popular in the south. A ceramic pot, called an *olla*, simmering with beans is a common sight in Mexican kitchens. Refried beans are actually only fried once. After they have been cooked until soft, they are mashed, and cooked again in a pan with additional ingredients.

Ingredients

250 g dried pinto beans, sorted and rinsed

Water

1 large onion, chopped and divided

1 tablespoon vegetable oil

2 cloves garlic, minced

Salt to taste

Tools

Kitchen scales

Measuring jug and spoons

Stockpot

Mixing spoon

Colander

Frying pan

Steps

1. Place the beans and half of the chopped onion in a stockpot. Add enough water to cover them by about 3 to 5 centimetres.

2. Bring the beans to the boil on a high heat, then reduce the heat and simmer covered for about 2 hours until the beans are soft.

3. Drain the beans in the colander, retaining the liquid in a measuring jug.

4. In a frying pan, heat the oil. Add the other half of the chopped onion and cook for about 6 to 8 minutes. Add the garlic and cook for around 1 minute more.

5. Add the drained beans and salt. Mash the beans with the back of a spoon to break them up. Pour in the cooking liquid a little at a time until the beans become a smooth paste.

Makes 6 servings
Time: 2 hours 30 minutes

Quick tip

Sometimes dried beans need to be sorted and cleaned before you use them. Pour the beans onto a baking tray, and pick through them to remove any odd-looking ones. Then rinse them well in cold water in a sieve to fully clean them before cooking.

luten free **V**egan **V**egetarian

Red salsa

Red tomatoes are the base of many salsas. Mexicans use the fresh flavours of salsa to add a kick to foods at home, in restaurants, or at street stalls all over the country. Use your salsa to top tacos or as a dip for tortillas.

Ingredients

4 medium tomatoes, diced
½ medium onion, diced
2 tablespoons chopped green chillies (or to taste)
1½ teaspoons garlic powder
1½ tablespoons lime juice
4 to 5 sprigs fresh coriander, chopped
Salt to taste

Tools

Knife
Chopping board
Measuring spoons
Mixing spoon
Bowl

Steps

1. Combine all of the ingredients in a bowl and mix well.

2. Allow to sit for about an hour or more at room temperature for the flavours to combine.

Makes 4 to 6 servings as a garnish for tacos or other Mexican dish
Time: About 10 minutes

Gluten free **D**airy free

Vegetarian **V**egan

VARIATION

There is no exact recipe for salsa. The amount of each ingredient used is up to you. If you want the salsa hotter or milder, add more or less chilli. If you love the taste of coriander, feel free to add more. You can even add in some sweetcorn, mango, or pineapple. It's up to you!

Guacamole

Avocados were new to the Spanish settlers. They called guacamole, a mixture of avocados and other native ingredients, the "butter of the poor". In Mexico, it is used as a topping for tacos and other Mexican dishes. You can also dip tortilla chips into it and enjoy it as a snack. Guacamole turns brown if left exposed too long, so serve it soon after you make it.

Ingredients

2 ripe avocados

½ medium onion, diced

1 medium tomato, diced

1 tablespoon chopped green chillies

4 to 5 sprigs fresh coriander, chopped

1 tablespoon lime juice

Salt to taste

Tools

Knife

Chopping board

Spoon

Fork

Mixing spoon

Steps

1. Cut the avocados in half, remove the stone, and scoop out the insides into a bowl.

2. With the back of a fork, mash the avocado until smooth, but chunky.

3. Add the diced onion, diced tomato, chillies, coriander, lime juice, and salt. Mix well.

4. Put in a bowl for serving with tacos or another Mexican dish.

Quick tips

A ripe avocado is soft to the touch on the outside. If you buy an avocado when it is hard, you will need to wait for a few days before using it.

How to cut an avocado:

- Cut it in half from top to bottom. Twist the two sides apart.

- To remove the stone, hit the pit with the knife, being very careful to make sure your hand isn't in the way. Twist the knife to remove the stone.

- Scoop out the soft flesh inside with a spoon.

Makes 4 to 6 servings as a garnish for tacos
Time: About 10 minutes

 Dairy free **G**luten free

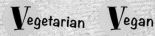 **V**egetarian **V**egan

Limeade

On a hot day in Mexico, there's nothing like a tall, icy drink to cool you down. Limeade, or *limonada* in Spanish, is one of Mexico's most popular beverages. This refreshing drink goes well with many Mexican meals. Double or even triple the quantities if you want to serve a larger crowd on an especially hot summer day!

Ingredients

100 g sugar
1.2 litres water, divided
5 to 6 limes for juicing
Ice
1 lime for garnish

Tools

Saucepan
Mixing spoon
Juicer
Bowl
Sieve
Jug
Glasses
Knife
Chopping board

Steps

1. In a small saucepan, combine the sugar and 250 ml of water. Bring to the boil and simmer until all of the sugar is dissolved. Take off the heat to cool.

2. Juice the limes into a bowl. Pour the juice through a sieve to remove any pulp and seeds. You should have about 180 ml of juice.

3. In a jug, combine the sugar water, lime juice, and the rest of the water. Stir well.

4. Pour into glasses over ice. Cut the last lime into slices or wedges to decorate the edge of the glasses.

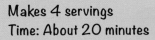

Dairy free   **G**luten free

Vegetarian   **V**egan

Makes 4 servings
Time: About 20 minutes

Dulces Mexicanos (Mexican sweets)

Desserts are a chance to enjoy the sweet side of Mexico. Ice cream and fruit ices are a cool treat after an especially fiery dish. Puddings and custards are a satisfying end to a meal. Sweets and chocolates are enjoyed for celebrations.

Flan

Flan is a popular Mexican custard. It cooks in a water bath in the oven. Traditionally, it is made in a special pan, called a bain-marie. But you can set a pie plate into a baking pan with high sides.

Ingredients	Tools	
225 g sugar	Saucepan	Kettle
4 large eggs	Spatula	Electric hand
2 (170-g) tins evaporated milk	23-cm round glass baking dish	mixer
		Kitchen foil
1 (400-g) tin sweetened condensed milk	Baking tray with high sides	Knife
		Serving dish
2 teaspoons vanilla extract		

Steps

1. Preheat the oven to 180°C.

2. Heat the sugar in a saucepan on medium heat until it begins to turn brown. Stir frequently with a spatula until it becomes caramel syrup, for about 10 minutes.

3. Carefully pour the syrup into the glass baking dish. Tilt the dish so the caramel completely covers the bottom and most of the sides. Set aside to cool.

4. Beat the eggs with a mixer in a large mixing bowl until well combined. Add the milks and vanilla extract and beat until smooth.

5. Pour the egg and milk mixture into the baking dish. Cover with kitchen foil.

6. Bring a kettle full of water to the boil and carefully transfer the water to a teapot.

7. **CAUTION:** Ask an adult to perform this step. Set the baking dish into a baking tray with high sides and place in the oven. Carefully pour the boiling water into the baking tray so it comes halfway up the sides of the dish.

8. Bake for 50 to 60 minutes. Test the centre with a skewer or knife. If it comes out clean, then it is cooked through.

9. Carefully remove the baking tray from the oven. With the baking dish still in its water bath, leave it to cool for about 1 hour.

10. Place the flan in the refrigerator to cool completely for a few hours.

11. To remove the flan, run a knife around the sides. Cover the flan with a serving plate and carefully flip the flan and plate over. Wiggle the baking dish to remove the flan.

12. Slice into wedges to serve.

Makes 8 servings
Time: About 1 hour 30
     minutes, plus a few
     hours to cool

Gluten free

Vegetarian

VARIATION

Add some other Mexican flavours to your flan. For cinnamon flan, add ½ teaspoon of ground cinnamon. For orange flan, add 1 teaspoon of orange zest (use a grater to make tiny strips from the peel of an orange).

Rice pudding

This is a simple, sweet Mexican pudding called *arroz con leche*, which literally means "rice with milk". Experience the warmth of Mexico with this comforting dessert.

Ingredients

500 ml water
200 g medium-grain white rice
1 teaspoon ground cinnamon
720 ml whole milk
150 g sugar
100 g raisins

Tools

Kitchen scales
Measuring jug and spoons
Saucepan
Mixing spoon

Steps

1. In a saucepan, combine the water, rice, and cinnamon. Bring to the boil on a high heat. Then turn the heat down to low, cover, and cook for about 15 minutes until all the water is absorbed.

2. Stir in the milk and sugar. Bring to the boil again over a medium-high heat. Then turn the heat to low, and cook uncovered for about 15 more minutes until the pudding has thickened. Stir frequently so that the milk and rice do not stick to the bottom of the pot.

3. Stir in the raisins.

4. Serve the pudding warm or chilled.

Gluten free   **V**egetarian

Makes about 4 to 6 servings
Time: About 30 minutes

Glossary

Tools

chopping board flat work surface that protects worktops from knife marks when cutting food

colander bowl-shaped tool with holes for draining liquid from foods

frying pan pan with a long handle and low sides for use on the hob

grater flat metal tool with small blades used to cut foods into small strips

grill device on a cooker that cooks food from above

juicer tool that helps remove the juice from fruits

kitchen scales device used to measure the weight of food ingredients

ladle serving spoon with a bowl-shaped scoop

measuring jug and spoons A measuring jug is marked with lines along the side to measure liquids. Measuring spoons come in different sizes to help you measure accurate amounts.

saucepan pan with a long handle, lid, and high sides for use on the hob

sieve utensil with a bowl-shaped wire or plastic mesh held in a frame, used for straining liquid from foods

spatula type of utensil with a flat end. Some spatulas are used for mixing, spreading, and scraping the sides of pots and bowls. Others are used for flipping food or removing it from the pan.

stockpot large, round metal pot with handles on each side and a lid for use on the hob

whisk tool used to break down ingredients and bring air into a mixture

Terms

boil	heat a liquid until bubbles rise to the surface
casing	outer covering of a sausage
char	cook until blackened
condiment	food that adds additional flavour served alongside a dish
dice	cut into small pieces (smaller than chopping, but bigger than mincing)
dissolve	become a part of a liquid
frothy	filled with lots of bubbles
garnish	add food as a decoration to a dish
grill	cook under a grill
marinate	soak in a liquid and spices to add flavour
mince	cut into very fine pieces
native	from a certain region
pulp	edible parts of a citrus fruit
puree	grind or mash ingredients until smooth
sauté	cook in a pan with a little fat, such as oil or butter
simmer	cook over low heat so that the liquid bubbles gently, but does not boil
to taste	amount that tastes best to you
whisk	beat quickly with a whisk to break down ingredients and bring air into a mixture
zest	peel of an orange or other citrus fruit

Find out more

Books

Angry Aztecs (Horrible Histories), Terry Deary (Scholastic, 2008)

Aztec (Eye Witness) (Dorling Kindersley, 2011)

Mexican Food Made Simple, Thomasina Miers (Hodder and Stoughton, 2010)

Mexico (Been There!), Annabel Savery (Franklin Watts, 2011)

Mexico (Countries Around the World), Ali Brownlie Bojang (Raintree, 2012)

DVDs

Lost Treasures of the Ancient World: the Aztecs and the Mayans (A Journey Back in Time), (Cromwell, 2003)

Moctezuma, Aztec Ruler, The British Museum (Quantum Leap Group, 2009)

Websites

Food Standards Agency
www.food.gov.uk/multimedia/pdfs/kitchen-check-yppack.pdf
Play these fun puzzles to help you stay safe in the kitchen.

The eatwell plate
food.gov.uk/scotland/scotnut/eatwellplate/#.UevoDNKsiSo
This site describes a healthy, balanced way to get all the
nutrients you need in the right proportions.

National Geographic Kids: Mexico
kids.nationalgeographic.com/kids/places/find/mexico/
View videos, look at maps, and read lots of information
on this interactive site.

Time for Kids: Mexico
www.timeforkids.com/destination/mexico
Visit this site to take a sightseeing tour of Mexico, learn
some Spanish, and learn how children spend their day.

Further research

If this book gave you a taste for Mexican food, there are
many more Mexican cookbooks you could look at. You
could also locate Mexican restaurants in your own town
or city to try a bite of authentic Mexican dishes.

You may also be curious about Mexico's history and
culture. Visit your local library and ask a librarian to
help you learn more. Or ask a parent to help you look
up websites for recipes, museums, or other information
about Mexico.

Index